Now I Am Home

EILEEN DISTASIO-CLARK

With Great Love and Appreciation to Those Who Have and Do Bless My Life.

My Family:

Joseph DeStasio Sr. & Miriam Lucille Baragone DeStasio, My Late Parents.

Andrea Jean DeStasio McIntosh, My Older Sister and Their Families.

Joseph DeStasio Jr., My Younger and Only Brother and Their Families.

Donna Marie DeStasio Wagner, My Younger Sister and Their Families.

My Children:

Eileen, Rebekah, Rachel, S. Michael,

Jennifer, Sharon, Tara, Stephanie,

Apryll, Mikaelah, & M. Trevor

and THEIR Families!!

ACKNOWLEDGEMENTS

First and foremost, I express, deeply, my sincere gratitude to our Heavenly Father for blessing me with the gift and talent of writing! I know I could not do what I do without His assistance.

I also want to acknowledge and express gratitude to the members of my birth family—Joseph Sr., Miriam, Andrea, Joseph Junior, and Donna. All the experiences of my childhood years, experiences that taught me so very much and enabled me to reveal my true self to myself, came about through my experiences and relationships with them.

And, of course, it goes without saying, but I will say it anyway: I also want to acknowledge and note my gratitude to my children, Eileen, Rebekah, Rachel, S. Michael, Jennifer, Sharon, Tara, Stephanie, Apryll, Mikaelah, and M. Trevor, and their families! Through multiple things they said to me, over multiple years, I finally came to the realization that

Heavenly Father gave me the gift of writing and opened the doors to these experiences because He knew that by sharing them with others, others could feel His love too.

And He definitely wants us all to know that He, Heavenly Father, Heavenly Mother, and Jehovah truly do loves us!!!

INTRODUCTION

There are sixteen books in this series, which I refer to as *"The Ellie Series."* All of the characters in these stories portray real people from my life. The main characters depict the members of my family: Daddy is my daddy; Mommy is my mommy; Jeannie is my older sister; Junior is my brother; Maria is my younger sister, and Ellie is me. Now, those are not our actual first names, but they do reference us.

The first story in the series presents our Heavenly Father's Plan of Salvation and takes place in the Pre-Earth World. Now, of course, because we all—when we were born—received what is known as The Veil of Forgetfulness, I do not actually remember everything from or about the Pre-Earth World, but I do know about and understand it from much study and worship as a member of The Church of Jesus Christ of Latter-Day Saints, and memories restored to me through the Holy Spirit. So, from this story, there is much truth to be learned.

The last story in the series is set in the Post-Mortal World, and presents a depiction of what happens to us after this life. Again, because I have not gone there yet, I cannot say I 'remember' this. But, I have also learned about the Post-Mortal World from much study and worship as a member of The Church of Jesus Christ of Latter-Day Saints.

All of the other stories are based on true events from my life; events that actually occurred when and how they are depicted in these stories. I chose these events because they are among the many occurrences in my life that presented—or revealed that which I already knew without having to be taught—Principles of Eternal Truths.

Also, I chose these events as the settings for my stories because they depict wonderful learning moments from my childhood and adolescent years, lessons that have blessed and benefited me throughout the whole of my life and will forever continue to do so. Also, through these great truths and their consequences in my life, I have been able to share them with many others, whose lives have also been blessed by them.

So, please, read and enjoy, then care and share the messages and stories with others!!

Now, there are also a couple of things you can look for:

In each story, the title of the previous story is presented in *italicized* form, the title of the next story is presented in *Capitalized Italicized* form, and the title of the story being read is presented in **emboldened** form.

Also, every story has at least one word that is uncommon or 'created.'

So, as you read, search, find, and have fun!

NOW I AM HOME

Never again!! Nope! Never!! Once was more than enough! Never! Nope! Never again!

'What are you talking about?' you may be wondering.

Well, I can clear that up for you. Those were Ellie's words about camp, the camp she attended when she was ten-years-old, the summer between fifth and sixth grades. Now, get me not wrong, Ellie loved to go camping, with her family. But Camp Fire Resident Camp? That was different, a difference she did not appreciate. It was not the camp, itself, nor was it the activities. She liked all of those. It was just that... well... mmmm... she... I have an idea. I will just tell you her story and you can figure out for yourself why Ellie decided that she would never again go to a resident camp.

It was a beautiful, bright and sunshiny day in mid-July! Ellie was up, dressed, packed, and ready to go. She even had her stuff in the car before breakfast was ready. She probably would have preferred to just leave without eating breakfast because breakfast that day was scrambled eggs.

Ellie hated scrambled eggs! Actually, Ellie hated eggs, no matter how they were prepared.

In fact, Ellie hated eggs even more than she hated pancakes, which she hated even more than she hated cereal, which she hated ever more than she hated oatmeal, and she thought there was nothing she could hate more than oatmeal! But then, that was what Ellie thought about just about everything edible. When it came to food, Ellie could count on less than two hands the things she actually liked. Now, you may be wondering what those foods were, and why she hated food so much. Well, I will tell you, at least as best I can.

I know she liked lemons (she ate those the way most people eat oranges), nuts and berries, tomatoes (if they came fresh from the garden), mushrooms (especially if they were hand-picked from the field), and one or two kinds of fish, sometimes. That was about it!

***Side Note:** As Ellie grew and changed, so did her tastes—changed that is, not grew. In fact, as she got older and especially when farmers changed the way they farmed, she liked food even less, and that included the things she had liked. So, it was not too surprising that some of the few things she actually did like when she was young, like fish. She actually did not like it anymore when she was older. But there were one or two things that she had never tasted when she was younger, like kiwis and clementines, that she realized she did like when she was older and tasted them. Still, Ellie and food were not friends, never had been, were not then, are not now, and never will be!! Now, back to the other side.

"I do not want scrambled eggs!" Ellie said with firm resolve, sitting down on the chair that was her designated seat, at the dining table. "I will not eat them!"

"You will," Mommy countered, "if you want to go to camp."

"What?!" Ellie bellowed, her eyes as wide as the moon, well, not really, the emotion was sufficient to spur a bellow, but the eyes were probably only as wide as Daddy's wedding ring (Ellie had small eyes). "You would not really keep me home from camp; would you?" she asked, as Mommy put her plate, with only one egg on it, on the table, in front of her.

"What do you think?" Mommy asked, with a tone that suggested it was not really a question but an 'Eat that egg, NOW!' kind of command.

Ellie put on her best pouty face and mumbled, with frustration, "Oh, baloney feathers," as she picked up the fork and, using it like a broom, 'swept' the egg around the plate. They were just 'baby sweeps' at first and only moved the bits of egg a tab bit. But, as Ellie became more frustrated, even the smell of the egg, which made her feel sick, made her more upset, she started 'sweeping' a little harder and faster, and faster and harder, and har… well, you get the idea, she kept 'sweeping' until a little bit of the egg accidentally, hmmm, was it truly accidentally? Well, until a bit of the egg ended up down on the floor. That gave Ellie an idea, an idea she often got when she did want to eat what she was supposed to be eating! Anyway, she began to sweep the plate again. But…

Seeing what Ellie had done, she had done it many times before, and knowing she knew what Ellie was doing, Mommy said, in her scolding voice, "Ellie! Pick that up! Throw it away! And do not make any more of your egg fall to the floor! Eat… that… egg!! You will not leave this table until you do!"

Ellie 'stormed' off her chair, picked the bit of egg up off the floor, threw it in the garbage can, and then went back to the table to 'choke down' the rest of the egg. Clearly, she was not happy about having to eat that egg.

In fact, if it had been any other day, she probably would have chosen to just sit there until the Atlantic

Ocean dried up and the Rocky Mountains fell down, rather than eat that egg. But it was not any other day; it was the day that camp began, and she really wanted to go to camp. So, with genuine choking, Ellie 'choked down' the egg.

Once done with breakfast, Ellie ran upstairs to brush her teeth, comb her hair, and get her shoes, which of course, she had not put on when she got dressed. Because Ellie does not like to wear shoes, she never puts them on unless and until she has to, and only at the last minute, the very last minute, which is what she actually thought it was, the last minute, the very last minute, before leaving for camp.

"Okay," Ellie announced as she slid down the banister and landed on the landing, "I am ready! Let us go!!"

"We will," Daddy replied as he finished the last bite of his eggs, "when we are all ready."

Knowing that 'all' meant everyone, Daddy, Mommy, Jeannie, Junior, Maria, and her, and seeing that she was the only one ready, Ellie huffed as she jumped from the stairs landing, over the bottom step, to the floor. Ellie puffed as she hopped across the living room to Daddy's favorite overstuffed chair. Ellie blew the house down, the house that Daddy and Junior had built out of playing cards, as she plopped herself down, where? In his overstuffed chair? No, on the floor, her favorite place to sit! Aside from the chair where the card house had been.

"Oh, fiddle-faddle!" Ellie moaned as she looked at the pile of cards. "Why do I always do stuff like that?"

"That is a good question," Jeannie said, as she sat down on their comfy couch, to put her shoes on. "Why do you?" she asked.

Ignoring the question, for which Ellie really did not know the answer, and seeing that Jeannie was putting on her shoes, she asked, with renewed excitement, "Are you ready to go?"

"Yep," Jeannie replied, "and so are Junior, Maria, and Mommy."

"Oh, good!" Ellie exclaimed, hustling to pick up all the cards. Then, jumping up off the floor and heading hastily for the door, she said, "I am going to wait in the car." And that was what she did!

Now, even though it really did not take long for everyone else to get to the car too, Ellie was sure she had been waiting for a ridiculously long time! But, once everyone was in the car and Daddy was starting the engine, that did not matter anymore. They were on their way and that was good!

Since it was not even ten miles from their house to Camp Adahi, where Camp Fire Resident Camp was being held, and it was a Monday morning after rush hour, and most of the drive was in the country, it did not take them very long to get there. Now, to Ellie, that was both really good and not so good. She definitely was excited to get to camp, but she would have preferred to have had more time to look at all the horses in the country pastures. Still, once they arrived at Adahi, Ellie was just so happy that there was no way she could be sad.

Daddy pulled into the parking lot where all the campers were being checked in and found an open space right next to the exit. That was pretty nice because with all the cars that were there, being so close to the exit made it easier for them to get out of the parking lot after Ellie had been checked in and was being escorted by the camp leader of her group, to the 'cabin' to which she had been assigned.

As Ellie looked around the 'cabin,' which was not really a cabin, she felt a twinge of something she could not identify. And she did not know why she was feeling... whatever it was she was feeling... but it did not feel good. Was it because of the 'cabin'?

'The cabin?' you may be questioning. 'Why would the cabin make her feel... whatever it was she feeling?' Well, let me explain that to you.

The four steps leading up to the 'door' of the cabin, which was not a real door, were made of the same kind of wooden planks used to build decks. Ellie did not like the spaces between the planks. She remembered getting her foot stuck in steps like that when she was a little girl. A very little girl. And, she remembered that it hurt!! A lot!!!!

The floor of the cabin was wood too, which Ellie did like, but the walls and roof were canvas, the old kind of canvas that stank when it got wet. In reality, it was a canvas tent on a wooden platform, not a real cabin, but it was also not a real tent! So, Ellie decided it was a 'cabent'—cab for cabin and ent for tent—'cabent!' And, to her, that was NOT where you stayed when you went camping! Now, let us go inside.

Inside the 'cabent,' there were four cots, one in each corner. That was all. But that was okay because, as everyone knows, when you go camping, you live out of a suitcase. However, Ellie was not excited about the cots. To her, camping meant sleeping in a sleeping bag, on the floor, in a tent that was set up on the ground!

So, was that why Ellie was feeling, whatever it was she was feeling, that really did not feel good, but did not really feel bad enough to feel bad? She could not tell herself that it was, nor could she tell herself that it was not because she did not know.

After getting 'settled in,' all that meant was rolling open their sleeping bags onto their cots and sliding their suitcases under their cots, all the campers were called together for an orientation meeting. The planned activities, which everyone was excited about, were explained to them, and their chores, which no one was excited about, were assigned to them. Ellie's group was assigned the latrine, which after seeing it Ellie deemed appropriately named!

It was disgusting! It was gross! It was... well, let me just say, Ellie was so sickened by it that she used it as little as possible for the entire week, all five days, which meant she did not eat very much either. Then again, as picky as she was about eating, she would not have eaten much anyway. Now, back to the latrine. Uh… that does not sound… oh well, let us just go!

It was her group's chore that day to wipe down the 'seats' in the two outhouses, the faucets in the two showers, and the twelve cold-water sinks, there were not even any hot water faucets on those sinks that were outside under a roof. Even after they were done cleaning them, they still were dirty and yucky at least that was how they looked. I guess the leaders knew that though, because the girls did not have to go back and clean them again, and that made all the girls very happy!!

The better part of that day was the hike everyone took all around Camp Adahi after all the chores were done. That was fun, especially for Ellie, who not only loved to be outdoors, but who loved to walk, and walk, and wal… well, you know where this is going. It was the best part of the day, as far as she was concerned. But then again, even that seemed somehow, in some way, different than walks usually felt for her. But why? Again, she did not know.

The worst part of the day, well, next to cleaning the latrine, was dinner, and not just because of the food, but also because they ate in a mess hall. *Gee*, Ellie thought, with mounting irritation, as she was served her dinner by one of the cooks. 'You would think that they think that we joined the army.'

You see, that was another thing that was out of place in Ellie's mind. When they—the Stations, Ellie's family—went camping, they cooked everything over an open campfire. It was fun! It smelt good! It even, sometimes, almost, kind of, in a way, just about tasted good enough to eat! But there they were, in a mess hall, being served slop, at least that is what Ellie thought it looked like.

Did she eat it? Nope! She just sat at the table with everyone else in her group, waiting for them to finish eating. When the others were done and were taking their plates to the kitchen, Ellie took hers too, dropping the slop in a trash can that stood by the kitchen door.

Now, they did have a campfire later that night, and every night, which ended with taps, suggesting all the more to Ellie that they, the leaders, must have thought that they—the girls—had joined the army. But Ellie did not care too much about that because she really did enjoy sitting around the campfire, singing songs, telling stories, and even, just before taps, reading one scripture from the Bible! That was something unexpected but pleasingly pleasant to Ellie. And, she noticed that when the scripture was read, she felt good, better than she had throughout the whole of the day. Then when she laid down for the night, after saying her prayers, and while unsuccessfully trying to fall asleep, she began to think about the camping trip that her family had taken to French Creek State Park, the summer before.

Side Note:** Of all the talents Ellie had, the ability to sleep, or at least to sleep well, like most people, was not one of them. Most nights, if she could sleep at all, it took her more hours to fall asleep than she had hours left to stay asleep. So, typically, while trying to fall asleep, Ellie contented herself by creating mental fantasies, reliving memories, or teaching herself new things, or... well, okay, I am pretty certain you know what I mean, she contented herself with thoughts and imaginations. Now, back to the other side. That side being Ellie's family's camping trip to French Creek, when Ellie was nine-years-old, the summer between her fourth and fifth grade school years.

It was early in the evening, on a warm Friday, early in June, when they arrived at the check-in booth at French Creek State Park. It was their first camping trip, well, a camping weekend of the summer, and all of the Stations were feeling quite elated. Well, almost all; Daddy, Ellie, Junior, and Maria were elated, but Mommy and Jeannie, who did not enjoy camping as much as they enjoyed vacationing in a cabin, were not quite as thrilled. But, as they approached their campsite, they did become more excited.

It was the most awesomely cool campsite ever! The best in the whole park, or any park! At least according to Ellie and Junior. It was at the end of the little road that led from the park entrance to the creek. That meant there would be no one camping across the road from them, because there was nothing but trees, trees, lots of trees on that side of the road, and the campsite aside of theirs was separated from them by a bunch, a bunch, a big bunch of trees. But even better than all of that, their campsite was right next to the creek, and that was where they liked to be. The sound of the rushing water was inviting during the day, when they wanted to explore, and soothing at night, when they wanted to sleep.

As soon as Daddy stopped the car, put on the brake, and opened his door to get out, Ellie and Junior jumped over the seat and scampered out the door. They ran all over the campsite, examining everything, the table, the firepit, the big open space where they would be putting their tent, the trees, the bushes, the… well, I think you get it, they looked over this, that, and everything else! About the time they were done exploring their campsite, Daddy finished unpacking the car and called for everyone to come help put up the tent and unpack the stuff that needed to be unpacked.

With everyone—and I do mean everyone, that is Daddy, Mommy, Jeannie, Ellie, Junior, and Maria— everyone working together, it did not take long for the tent to be up and firmly staked, the sleeping bags (and cots for Daddy and Mommy) to be placed in place inside the tent, the food cooler to be tucked under the end of the table, and the camp stove to be set up on the table, just above the cooler. Then, when all of that was done, they got their camp chairs, set them up around the fire pit and sat down together to enjoy the cool, comfortable breeze that was blowing through the trees, while they planned out, or at least made a list, of the things they wanted to do that weekend. It must have been a pretty good list because they actually were able to do everything they wanted to do, and that was something that did not always happen.

Because, by the time they finished all their planning, it was a little later than their usual dinner time, they decided to just roast marshmallows and chestnuts over the campfire and have those with some fresh squeezed lemonade. And yes, of course, Ellie ate the rest of the lemons after the juice was squeezed out of them. Then, still sitting around the campfire, they sang some songs, told some stories, and shared some jokes, until the fire, which had been pretty huge when they first started it, burned down into little, glowing embers. Then, one by one, with Daddy being the last one, since he was the one to water the embers in order to prevent another fire from starting, they all settled into their sleeping bags in the tent, said their prayers, shared their 'Good-nights,' and wandered off into dreamland.

Early, or not so early for some of them, the Stations arose and began their day with breakfast, which was cereal, which of course, Ellie complained about. Now, knowing that she would probably not be able to do everything she wanted to do if she did not eat her breakfast, she chose to eat it without complaint, though it was quite a struggle. But then, when was it not?!

After breakfast, they spent the rest of the morning hiking on the trails that traversed the park. They enjoyed the beautiful trees and bushes, the peaceful scenery, and the challenging hills. They raced each other down the hills and across the meadows. They talked, sang, joked, and laughed together. It was a great morning!

After lunch, Daddy took Jeannie, Ellie, Junior, and Maria swimming in the creek. Mommy sat by the creek side, enjoying her crossword puzzles, as she watched the rest of them slipping, sliding, splashing, and dashing over the rocks, through the water, and down the waterfall, which was tiny enough to be safe, but big enough to be fun. After their swimming adventure, they all went to the playground and swung on the swings, slid down the sliding board, and spun on the merry-go-round. It was a fantastic afternoon!! In fact, the whole weekend was fabulous!

But how could it not have been, Ellie thought, snuggled in her sleeping bag, on the cot, in the cabent, *we were outside; we were camping; we were playing; but best of all, we were together!*

As Ellie finally began to wander off into dreamland, she noticed that, while she had felt good, remembering the camping trip to French Creek State Park, she was not feeling that feeling anymore. She was again feeling that twinge of something she could not identify. She still did not know why she was feeling… whatever it was she was feeling… but she did know that it was the same feeling that she had been feeling all day. In fact, even though she felt it from time to time throughout the week, it was not until she went home that she finally understood what she had been feeling and why. Hmmm. Maybe I should fast forward and tell this story in reverse. It could make more sense that way. Yeah! Let us do it!!

Okay, so the week ended on Friday afternoon. But it was not Friday afternoon when Ellie was packed and ready to go. She took care of all of that Friday morning as soon as she got up! So, when it was time to go, she was one of the first ones to leave, and that felt good!

All the way home, which did not take long, and all through dinner, which was homemade pizza and milkshakes, Ellie told her family about all the things they did at camp. She started with the yukky stuff, like cleaning the latrine and eating slop in the mess hall, and about sleeping on a cot in a 'cabent.'

Side Note:** Ellie did not even have to tell them what that was. They were so used to Ellie's word creations that they actually figured that one out for themselves. Now, back to the other side.

She told them about the night they slept outside, on the ground, under the trees. She was really happy about that, because that was 'real camping!' After some of the older girls had helped the leaders cover the ground with plastic tarps so the sleeping bags would not get wet from the dew, they spread their sleeping bags out on the tarps, all aside of each other, in one super long row and put their pillows on top of them. She told them how everything was going really well, until...

"I got in my sleeping bag," Ellie began, in story-telling mode, "closed my eyes and said a little prayer. Then, just as I was about to lie down, Alexis, the girl next to me on my left side, yelled, 'STOP! There's a big spider on your pillow!'"

"I jumped up, looked at the spider and froze! I could not move; I could not talk; I could not do anything! Why, it was so big, it made Jupiter look like a ping-pong ball."

"Jupiter?" Daddy laughed. "A ping-pong ball?"

"A spider?" Jeannie chimed in, "As big as Jupiter?"

"Well," Ellie defended her exaggeration, "things always seem bigger when you get scared. I do not know what scared me more, the spider or the way Alexis yelled, but I sure do know that I sure did feel scared."

She continued to tell them how the leaders, with some of them climbing into the tree and some of them staying on the ground, took the whole web out of the tree. Fortunately, there were no other spiders in the web. That was good because if there had been, they would have fallen on the girls and maybe even gotten into their sleeping bags. That would have ruined the night for sure. Then again, for Ellie, it already had changed the night; she did not sleep very much at all, not that that was something new for her, but that night, all she could think about, was the spider!

Ellie also told them about the snake in the lake. "I will NEVER go swimming in a lake again!" she began with absolute conviction. "I did not like it anyway, because of all the mud and the muck, but now..."

Junior, who had become very enrapt by Ellie's spider adventure, moved closer to her so he would not miss a word about her snake in the lake tale. She continued, again in story-telling mode, "It was time for swimming lessons. I did not really want to get in the water. I know I cannot swim very good, but I did want to earn the swimming bead. So, I got in the water with everyone else. But then..."

Ellie stopped for a moment; she actually seemed to be a little uneasy. So, Jeannie sat down next to her as she began to continue. "The swim instructor lined all of us up about twenty-five feet away from the dock, that was what she told us. Then she said she wanted us to swim back to the dock. Well, Alexis went first and did a pretty good job. Laney and Drew followed and they swam really well. Then it was my turn, but I did not move. They kept telling me to come, but I could not move. The swim instructor asked me what was wrong, but I could not answer. I was scared."

"Why?" Mommy asked, with both curiosity and concern.

"There was something in the water. I felt it swim past me. When it came back, I could feel it going around my leg. That was when one of the swim instructors got in the water and swam over to me. She asked me what was wrong, but I still could not say anything, so I just pointed to the water. So, she put her goggles down over her eyes and went under the water, and she saw it."

"Saw what?!" Junior asked, almost sounding a little scared too.

"It was a snake, wrapped around my leg," Ellie said softly.

"WHAT!" Daddy, Mommy, Jeannie, Junior, and even Maria yelled in unison.

"Uh-huh," Ellie said, "and it was big, really big, bigger than that black pipe in the cellar, the one that goes outside!" Ellie paused for just a second, and then clarified, "Well, not that fat, but that long!"

"What did they do?" Jeannie asked with a tinge of alarm.

"When the lady that was in the water had come up, she told everyone else to get out of the lake. But she told me to stay very still. Now, she did not really have to tell me that; I was too scared to move anyway.

"After everyone was out of the lake, she went back under the water and that was when I felt the snake move off of my leg. I was still too scared to move, so she helped me get out of the lake. We did not go back to the lake for the rest of the week and I was glad. I am never going to go in another lake again!”

“Ellie,” Jeannie asked, “did you have any fun at camp?”

“Yeah, some,” she said. “I liked when we got to take a walk all around the camp. Alexis, Laney, Drew, and I were not assigned to do the basket weaving, so our leader said we could walk on the trail, but we had to stay on the trail. So, we did, and I did like that.

“And there was the day we learned archery. That was really fun!”

"What is archry?" Maria asked.

"Archery," Mommy corrected. "It is when you shoot arrows at a target."

"Like Robin Hood?" Junior questioned.

"Yeah," Ellie confirmed, "like Robin Hood." Continuing her explanation, she said, "We were all assigned a target, mine was the first one, on the left side of the row. They gave us a bow and showed us how to use it. Then they gave each of us ten arrows and let us shoot them at our targets.

"I did not think I did too good, because I only got three of them in the middle of the target, but the instructor said I did really good because I got all of them on the target. She said that was *something to be proud of.* She also said that I had good eye/hand coordination. I do not know what that is, but she was smiling when she told me that, so I figured it was something good."

"It is very good," Daddy assured her, "and you always have had real good eye/hand coordination. You can use your eyes and hands together do anything you want to do, and you do it very well."

"Well, it sounds like you had a pretty good week," Mommy said. Then, expecting a 'yeah, sure' kind of reply from Ellie, she asked, "So, do you want to go back to resident camp again next year?"

Ellie was quiet for a somewhat longer than usual moment. She looked down at the floor with a curious expression on her face, as if she was trying to figure out something. Finally, she looked up at Mommy, and then she looked at Daddy. She looked at Junior, then at Maria, then at Jeannie, then back at Mommy and said, simply, "No."

"No?!" Mommy responded with surprise, "Why not?"

"I… well…" Ellie began. She seemed to not really know how to answer that question.

Seeming to know the answer but wanting her to give it to them, Daddy asked, "Ellie, were the other girls nice to you?"

Again, Ellie looked down at the floor, but this time with an expression that seemed to suggest that, while she did know the answer to the question posed to her, she did not want to give the answer to them. Nonetheless, she did. And this is what she said.

"Well, I guess they were, some of them. Laney was pretty nice most of the time, but I felt really bad when she laughed at me. She was even making fun of me."

"Why?" Mommy asked sympathetically.

"Because I was singing the Scooby-Doo song, and when she asked me if I still watched that, and I told her I do, she started making fun of me. She said it was a little kid's cartoon and I was too old to still be watching it. Alexis and Drew got mad at her and told her to be quiet. They said they still watch it too. I felt a little better after that, but... I do not know. The whole week was different than what I thought it would be."

"How?" Daddy asked.

"Well, I had a funny feeling. I mean, not really funny. It was not a nice feeling, but I never could figure out what it was or why I felt it."

"When did you feel it?" Mommy asked.

"All the time, I guess," Ellie replied, but then added, "but, sometimes more than other times. Like, when we were taking walks around the camp. I liked the walk, but it was different somehow, not like when I walk with Daddy.

"And when we were in the mess hall, sitting at the table with the leaders, everyone was talking except me. I know that happens all the time, but... it made me feel like... like I was alone. I do not feel that way when I am with you, Mommy, and I do not talk."

Daddy stood up, took Ellie's hands, pulled her up to a standing position, and gave her an extra big, 'big hug.' He hugged her for a little while before explaining this to her, "Ellie, you are a sweet little lady who loves people a lot! But, I think, when you are not with us, what you feel is what we call homesickness."

"What is that?" Ellie asked.

"That means, when you are not with us, you miss us!" Daddy explained as he gave her another pretty big, 'big hug!' "And you miss us, your family, because you love us!!"

Well, now you have it, Ellie's story about camp. I wonder if you are wondering whether Ellie felt it was a good week or if it was a not-so-good week. I think if you asked her, especially now, she would tell you it was a 'not-so-good-very-good' week.

You see, the next day, the day after she had gotten home from camp, she was sitting in the little red wagon under the Catalpa tree. She thought about all the fun things she had done at camp, but she also thought about the strange feeling that she had had, the feeling that Daddy had called homesickness. As she did, she realized, not really for the first time ever, but in a way that she had not realized it before, that she loved being home more than she loved being anywhere else.

She loved the house they lived in! She loved the room she slept in! She loved the garden that Daddy planted in the back of the yard! She loved the hopscotch that Daddy painted on the pavement behind the house. She loved their Catalpa tree. She loved Daddy! And Mommy! And Jeannie! And Junior! And Maria! And their dogs, when they had one! And she loved *The Angels in Their Backyard Tree.*

Yes, Ellie loved home and her family, and that was where she was the most happy and comfortable. She knew, and maybe she always had known, that God puts us together in families because that is where we can be and should be most loved, blessed, and cared for. As she sat there and thought about the adventures she had already had in her life and considered the adventures to come, she realized that no matter where she went, what she did, or who she was with, she would always feel her happiest when she could tell herself, **now, I am home.**

ABOUT THE AUTHOR

Eileen DiStasio-Clark is the second oldest of four children. She is the mother of eleven children and grandmother to twenty-three grandchildren, to date. As a member of The Church of Jesus Christ of Latter-Day Saints, she serves in various positions, teaching, leading, and ministering to children, youth, and adults. Currently, she is also a Family History Missionary. Eileen established the Pursuit of Excellence Institute of Family Education, a non-profit organization focused on strengthening the family. Presently she holds an AA, a BA, and an MA in Clinical Psychology and is working on the completion of her Doctoral Degree.